A Food Truck Success Manual

Ten Moneysaving, Moneymaking, and Time Management Strategies For Starting a Food Truck Business

Gabe Ceniceros

A Food Truck Success Manual
By: Gabe Ceniceros

ISBN: 979-8-89443-879-5

Cover photo courtesy of the Arizona Daily Star

For contact information, please go to:
www.TheBlackTopGrill.com
or email: TheBlackTopGrill@outlook.com

Arizona Book Publishing
www.ArizonaBookPublishing.com

Awards & Recognitions

2014

- I began this journey with just a small food cart.
- 2015 to 2018 were trial and error stages, working very hard to create a successful food truck.

2018

- Wurst Festival, Phoenix, AZ, won recognition for 'Elotero Hotdog.'
- Chili Pepper Festival, Phoenix, AZ, won prizes for 'Chili Relleno Hotdog & Texan Quesadilla.'

2019

- Wurst Festival, Phoenix, AZ, won recognition for 'Shanghai Hotdog.'
- Voted 'Best Food Truck' by Restaurant Guru

2020

- Opened my Brick n Mortar store in Tucson, AZ
- Survived the Covid Pandemic
- Voted 'Best Food Truck' by Arizona Daily Star

2022

- Nominated 'Best New Tucson Restaurant'
- Button Brewhouse Tapas Competition, 1st Place
- Tapas winner by People's Choice
- Nominated for 'Best Hotdogs in Tucson'
- City of Gastronomy Certified Restaurant

2023

- Nominated for 'Tucson's Best Tacos'
- Nominated for 'Tucson's Best Street Corn'
- Was listed by Restaurant Guru as one of the Ten Best Fast-Food Restaurants in Tucson
- Voted Top Ten Food Trucks by Travelers Atlas
- Won First Place 'Judges Choice Award' at the Button Brewhouse Chili Cook-Off in Tucson

2024

- Nominated for 'Tucson's Best Tacos'
- Nominated for 'Northwest's Best Kept Secret'
- Listed in Monopoly Tucson Edition by Hasbro
- Local Marana Business of the Year

Introduction

On any given night in 2009, I would visit a small suburb of my hometown, Yuma, Arizona, to indulge in what I can only describe as a primitive version of a "Sonoran Hotdog." These delicious, unique, and distinctive hotdogs came from my favorite hotdog cart. These hotdogs were wrapped in bacon on a freshly baked bun with refried beans, tomato, onion, mayo, mustard, and whatever else the "creator of Dogs" might have decided to add that night.

It was every drunk and pothead's dream; however, this particular cart went even further with *killer refried beans and onions sautéed in mustard*, gourmet food-cart amazingness that I knew I would someday miss.

It became my go-to, and I made a point to stop there anytime I was in the area. However, one drunken night in 2009, I realized *I could do this line of work myself.*

I give full credit to the owner of that food cart for lighting my fire to start my own food truck eventually.

The food was so good, at times I still think about it.

The hotdogs were $3.00 a piece but well worth at least $5.00… so on that same night, I asked the owner, "How many hotdogs do you sell per week?"

He responded, "Oh, about seven hundred!"

That's what sealed the deal for me because I did the math. Seven hundred hotdogs a week at $3.00 each.

At that moment, a light turned on inside my head because on that cold drunken night in 2009, making $2,100.00 a week sounded like a heck of a lot of money.

I was like the classic story of a guy who was tired of working for idiot bosses and wanted to be his own boss but without much money in my pocket. However, I had resourcefulness, over 20 years in the restaurant industry, a love for food, and a lot of creativity.

Ironically, after working in the restaurant industry, at one point, I had visions of a cozy, air-conditioned, stress-free office job, but when I actually got "the job," I found myself missing the challenge and movement that the service industry had given me; something the challenge an office job could never provide, so I was most definitely ready to get out and go at it alone.

Fast forward to 2014, that's when I took the leap and purchased my own food truck. No overthinking, scared as hell, and with only a promise to myself to ride this out through thick or thin and see where this venture would take me. It's now 2024; after ten amazing years in business, I have yet to sell seven hundred hotdogs in a week, but my journey has been fruitful. I am creative by nature and strive to give people the same craving that the Sonoran hotdog vendor gave me back in 2009.

My food truck is called "The Blacktop Grill."

The name was created with two meanings.

Blacktop represents the paved streets of the city.

It also means a forbidden fruit, the black market, the back streets, not an average menu or a true hidden gem.

The Blacktop Grill still specializes in decadent hotdogs and cheesy quesadillas but offers an array of other fresh and exciting menu options.

I change the menu seasonally to keep it exciting and interesting, not only for myself but also for my customers, both new and returning.

We call our food style *Gourmet Comfort Food*, also known as *Mexican Fusion.*

Our food is fun, fresh, affordable, and exciting new combinations inspired by traditional Mexican cuisine, such as Blacktop's award-winning Elotero Hotdog, made with fire-roasted corn, house-made chipotle lime sauce with garlic sriracha spice, and queso cotija (ground white cheese).

Another exciting item is our extremely popular Mango Quesadilla, with melted mixed cheeses.

I took a small and basic hotdog truck and made it into an income-earning machine. It was not big, fancy, or anything like the trucks you see on TV, but I was able to make a living dispensing exciting yet simple food out of this hooptie (*which means, an old vehicle in rough condition).*

Despite being limited to a small space and too many health department regulations, I soon found myself walking away from "the man."

Over the years, I upgraded my truck to one that was much more appealing to the eye, modern, and most importantly, safer to work out of.

But remember, *bigger is not always better.*

In previous years, The Blacktop Grill garnered attention from multiple food shows, podcasts, and blogs, plus our menu items often received awards.

We recently built a "brick n' mortar" store with the same name in Tucson, AZ, and have grown quite a large "foodie following," so please come by and see us if you're ever in the area.

§§§§§

TV shows and movies show you the glitter and glam side of running a food truck, and this is where most people get excited. I know I did.

Some shows discourage potential entrepreneurs by outlining the gut-wrenching work involved.

Focusing on how difficult something like this can be is intimidating rather than motivating.

It goes without saying, the food truck business requires hard work, but if you've been given the proper direction and strategy you can do it. Being properly informed will save you from making huge mistakes that may cost hundreds, even thousands of dollars, and also hundreds of wasted hours.

§§§§§

I often get asked for advice and secrets on how I made my first truck a success and how one can start their own venture. That's the motivation for this book. The truth is, there are no secrets at all, but with a little creativity and some hard work, you can be well on the road to creating a successful food truck business that you can be proud of.

However, let me emphasize that if you don't like to work, think there is not going to be work involved, or are not ready or willing to do the work, PLEASE STOP READING NOW.

There are no shortcuts that are going to get you recognized or make the income you're hoping for overnight. You must be dedicated and in it for the long haul. So, if you're ready to start your new and exciting venture, this book will help you skip some of the mistakes I made, and the mistakes of others.

I'm going to provide you with information that will make for a smoother path to your start-up by saving you time, money, and energy. I'm including pointers, headache savers, and tricks of the trade that you just won't find anywhere else.

Over the years, I've seen many vendors come and go, new businesses never making it past the first year, at times starting after watching a food truck show on a network that got them excited, then never seeing them again at the end of the year.

I can't imagine all of the disappointments and broken hearts that come with failing at a business.

I want everyone willing to take the leap into the food truck industry to be successful. I want to help you to follow your passion and move forward.

That's my motivation, so if my knowledge can help you, then I'm willing to share. This book can be used as a reference guide through the process.

§§§§

This last story will show you what my journey looked like when I started and where I am now.

On my first day out, I had all the passion, all the motivation, the licenses, and my menu ready to go.

I couldn't wait to make hundreds of dollars!

I found a perfect spot on the campus of the local university where hundreds of students would walk by on their way to class. I had everything cooked and prepared for a line of hungry students but only served one item that first day out. I quickly realized that quitting my day job was not yet an option.

It went on like that for weeks only to realize that most college kids don't have a lot of extra money. I did make some sales here and there, but it wasn't enough to get excited about, especially after all the work involved in preparation to get the day started.

This struggle continued for a year, but I took a deep breath and faced it one day at a time.

Being new to this business I knew there would be a lot to figure out from day to day, adjustments to be made, and of course, mistakes.

One of my biggest mistakes, which I still feel embarrassed to talk about, was not passing my first health inspection on the fourth week. It was such a blow to the gut because I was already mentally drained from all the constant learning, the anxiety from all the little details, and all the work involved.

I wouldn't say it was negligence on my part but more of a lack of education and being a new food truck owner with so much on my plate already.

The local news does a segment on restaurants that don't pass inspection and guess who was on it just after the first few weeks into this venture.

Yup, you guessed it.

I think it would have been normal for anyone to throw in the towel after the first month I had, but instead, I promised myself I would not allow that to ever happen again and kept threading along.

Since then, The Blacktop Grill has passed every inspection with an excellent health rating.

I wouldn't go back and change anything.

Experiences like that humbled me and allowed me to appreciate the worth of a dollar. They have helped raise my standards, and through hard work, have shown me that strategizing, consistency, and perseverance are the ingredients for a well-oiled, successful money making-machine.

In my first year, I could have never imagined that I would be sitting down to write this book or have the knowledge to share my experience.

I didn't have mentors to help me, but I would have jumped all over a book like this.

I took it one day at a time through headaches and stresses that have allowed me to sit here today and give anyone such valuable advice.

This venture has been an amazing ride that has not only opened many doors for me but has also given me a vision for the future.

Even on days when motivation can't be found, and I have to dig deep, these experiences keep me moving forward. Yes, I have had my fair share of mistakes, which in turn have helped me get to this point by avoiding the same mistakes twice.

So now I am sharing the experiences I thought would be valuable to anyone with fire in their gut to start a food stand, cart, truck, or whatever.

I also want to highlight that through my many experiences,the numerous relationships I've made, the good reputation I've built, and the countless awards and acknowledgments that The Blacktop Grill received has thus far surpassed anything monetary I ever plan on making in the future; and that my friends, has been worth the entire struggle.

I hope that my guidance will help you on your journey, allowing a much smoother ride for your new venture, your pocketbook, and your sanity.

Bailee Rollins recommends The Blacktop Grill.
May 16, 2019 ·

The first time I had Blacktop Grill a friend bought it for me and I took it to go. I was driving in my car, pulled back the foil wrapping and took a bite. I thought to myself this is NOT car food, it deserves my attention. It was so incredibly delicious that I pulled over to finish it.

Great food · Creative cuisine

The Blacktop Grill

1 Comment

Table of Contents

Chap I: Don't Fall Prey to Reality TV

Owning your own food truck business can be a fun, exciting, and lucrative venture, but we've been made to believe by televised food shows that there is an instant success that comes with starting a food truck, *that you will* see *people lining up at your food truck parked on the street just waiting to try all your exciting creations.*

You may think your stoner's dream of a waffle with marshmallows in between two pizza slices and a special sauce will have people lined up for miles, but the reality is your Frankenstein creation isn't likely to do that.

Television shows glamourize and focus on one item of a food-truck business for entertainment purposes, but what they don't show you is all the hard work involved from the daily duties, the slow days that you make very little money, or the people you see walking away just because you don't have a lot of healthier options.

Yes, you should offer a menu with lots of different options, including healthy ones although some of you may not want to consider going overboard with those, but trust me when I say… *you will dip into a whole other demographic that is looking for these healthier bites*.

I'll get into the menu in another chapter, but my point here is not to get sucked into all the glam because if that's why you're thinking of starting, just know there is nothing glamorous about this line of work.

There is no silver bullet, meaning there is no one item that will make you millions and make you famous.

I have award-winning eats; each has always been a great seller that drew repeat customers. Even after I won awards, I thought these items would be my ticket to the lines waiting to try them, and although the items did get lots of traffic, there's never been one around the block.

In fact, in all my years in business, the only time I've ever had a line around the block was because I was the only food truck at a poorly planned parade, which left a lot of people starving, which wasn't fun at all.

The real reward comes from compliments that I get about our food, great reviews, and people who return to see us or those who visit because we were recommended by word of mouth or a Yelp review. This doesn't happen overnight, but you must get started to get there.

The goal is to get your name out into the world, and that starts with a good reputation that will eventually get you a consistent flow of customers.

That starts with a great menu and items, their presentation, and of course, taste. It also includes talking with each visitor with a smile and a great attitude and walking each person through your menu with the same enthusiasm, *every single day.*

Don't spend all your money on a logo and a food truck when you haven't even invested the time needed to create a high-quality product that will be dispensed from your rig.

It's also easy to get discouraged and want to walk away from it after a slow month or a string of struggles; they happen. I still have slow days and at times I struggle with certain things, but in my experience, the slow and the busy days balance out each other to allow a consistent income.

Even your favorite restaurants have slow days and daily struggles. So, no matter how popular or who you are, they are going to happen. These are just a few of the subjects I will be touching on.

This book will show you how to get returning customers, great reviews, and to begin building an excellent reputation. It's also meant to help you grow, reach your income goals, and use your time more effectively so that you don't lose your sanity, or your wallet in the process of your journey.

§§§§§

Summary:

- Don't be sucked in by the television glam.
- Having a couple of healthy food options will give you another demographic of customers.
- There is no silver bullet. Not one item or thing will gain you the popularity you think it will.
- Nothing happens overnight.
- Your goal is to get your name out to the world for a consistent flow of customers.
- Keep the same enthusiasm every single day.
- Slow and busy days balance each other so that you have a consistent income.

Chap II: Take Time With Your Menu

Your menu is your breadwinner, attention grabber, conversation starter, and the key to your bright future, or your demise. In my opinion, working on your menu is the number one priority, far before you even consider becoming a food vendor.

It is vital to put some thought and heart into it.

People can taste the love put into food. That is why you should take time to put that love into your menu. When focusing on a menu don't just throw it together for a quick dollar or be overanxious to get out and start serving publicly. Instead, take the time to get creative and make attention-grabbing menu items that excite you and your future customers. Take the time to create items with ingredients that are exciting and appear yummy. Your menu should offer a nice presentation and always use quality products. It just takes one incident of some bad food service to lose your reputation.

If you have a proven family recipe, such as your grandmother's 100-year-old chicken & waffles, or old Uncle Willy's fresh pulled-pork sandwiches, then you're ahead of the game. If not, I suggest you get a mouthwatering menu started right away.

Give some thought to what your specialty will be. If it's going to be some sort of fancy hamburger, focus on making an amazing burger menu, keeping most of the other items in the realm of burgers also.

You want to be known for one main thing.

What is it for you? Burgers, tacos, pulled pork?

Caution: Be aware that too many options won't give customers a sense of what your truck is about.

Having a specialty item allows you to make only a few fantastic products from your menu, and also helps simplify your preparation.

Think about the time it would take to prepare ten different items and never give any focus to just a few items, making them the best they can be.

Take the time with your main menu item(s) and their ingredients. Allow family or friends to taste test and be the critics of your food so that they can give you the feedback you need on what should be adjusted, what works, and what doesn't.

Take the time to watch food shows or try new restaurants for inspiration. Make it a point to try items that have exciting ingredients and could make sense for some of your menu items.

Exciting ingredients you find need not be in the same type of food they were originally used for but can also make sense on your burgers or tacos.

Take the time to produce a menu that flows and is simple. Simple is key. You don't need a large extravagant menu to succeed. An extensive menu will only triple your prepping time and make it harder for you during your busy hours to keep up with so many options. People go to a food truck for a quick and delicious bite. If they want to wait 30 minutes for a meal, why not go to a restaurant?

Consider 8-10 items max for your menu.

Use colorful words when describing your menu to give your customer a mouthwatering picture in their mind as they read through it, like fire-roasted corn, fresh-grated parmesan, crispy spinach, homemade lemon glaze, and double-chocolate cream. However, if you already have a menu you've worked hard on and are ready to test on the hungry public, great, but keep an open mind and be willing to adjust your menu if some of this advice hits home.

If you haven't started your menu, you should start as soon as possible. Don't be impatient or be the food vendor who throws a poorly thought-out menu together for a quick buck or because of your over-excitement to get out serving. The menu should be the most fun and exciting part of this whole process.

Your menu plays a big role in your day-to-day workload, as I have already explained.

To start, make an item or two a week.

Get some friends on board who will be honest about your creation and will give you constructive criticism and feedback. Take the time to taste the item and its ingredients. Be open to change to make it better and more exciting. You may find that some items just don't work, but that's all part of the fun and the experimentation.

You want an outsider's opinion, not just your own.

Outsiders will ultimately be your biggest food critics. They will be your bread and butter, so you want them to have a good experience by offering something they crave that will keep them coming back for more and also get them to recommend your food truck to all of their friends.

One big eye-opener I had since starting my food cart is thinking that people I know would be the ones supporting my business, and I know a lot of people! My point is that I can count on one hand the people I know who have stopped by for a meal. There's no bitterness on my part, but it's a big world, so it's not the people you know, it's the people you don't know who will keep you in business.

Some food truck myths claim, "You must have a 100% unique idea." That's false. You can serve a burger or even a taco, but the question to ask is, *what makes your food stand out?* Whatever your specialty or your secret touch is, the one thing I am sure of is that you must always use top-quality products. People can taste cheap but most of them are willing to pay top dollar for quality menu items.

My wife is my number one critic and biggest supporter. In our first year, we tried 150 combinations of different items with only a selected few making the cut. I keep an eye out for exciting combinations that I think will work as a topping. Most don't, some do, and when they do, it's like I've found a diamond or just hit a home run because now I have something that I can be confident serving, knowing that I took the time to find the perfect combination. The point is that we don't just use the first idea that comes to mind on our menu. We test and test until we've found a combination that makes sense and excites us. It's important to keep an open mind that your menu may still change several times before you get it perfect.

Remember, *Keep It Simple!*

Below are examples of two menus. Examine them and decide why you would choose them. These items are examples and don't necessarily make sense when used together. Your job is to come up with the type of cuisine that excites you, choose your best items, and make your own menu.

Menu A

Fried mushrooms $6

Fried asparagus $6

Chicken/Beef Sliders (4) $6

Grilled Cheese Sandwich $5

Hotdog $3 add bacon $2

Quesadilla $6

Burger $5 with cheese $6

Fries $4

Nachos $4 add jalapenos $1

Side of salsa $2

Drink $2

Cheesecake slice $3

Churros (2) for $3

Menu B

Chicken wings (12) $10

Side salad $5

Chips $3

Side of guacamole $4

Flatbread Pizza (12") $12

Chicken Pasta $14

Hummus $6

Large Salad $8

Drink $2

Which menu did you decide on?

You might think 'Menu A' would attract more people because of the options, right?

Although 'Menu A' has more options it would take extra time and extra money to prepare it and would leave you exhausted from the prep alone.

Another disadvantage with so many options is *that* it's not guaranteed that people will even order half of the items, which in the end amounts to wasted time and money in trying to just keep up with such an extensive menu. Here is the big kick. You should not try to make money off your smaller-priced items to reach your monetary goal for the day.

Let's add some cost projections.

Example from menu A:

Two orders of wings $20

Three nachos with jalapenos $10

Three hotdogs $9

Four sodas $8

Cheesecake $3

Summary: It takes 12 items to total $50.00,

Example from menu B:

Order of two flatbread pizzas $24

Order of chicken wings $10

Large salad $8

Four sodas $8

Summary: It takes 8 items to total $50.00.

Menu B has less items for the same amount.

In my opinion, the best way I've found to get the best bang for my buck is "Menu B." It is a more simplistic menu, and the time you spend prepping and shopping is cut in half. Also, notice the price points. You won't need as many of the smaller items for extra money if you focus on the quality of the higher-priced items that you carry. In other words, you can sell fewer items and make just as much, rather than selling a lot of small fillers.

For a saner approach, don't struggle to get all the little items. It's about quality, not quantity.

Remember, *Work Smarter, Not Harder*.

For example, if you are going to charge $6.00 for a taco, make it a taco that people will crave and feel they received their money's worth.

Take the time to do some food research for your best menu items to make it worth the higher price but be sure to make it a reasonable price point.

A rule of thumb is to take the price you spent to make your item and multiply it by four.

This should give you plenty of room for profit.

People pay for quality food, so if you are using quality products, real food lovers will happily pay.

Don't be discouraged by a cheap-ass person looking for a $1.00 hotdog from a gas station. Yes, they exist but give customers a quality $6.00 hotdog with well-thought-out creative toppings.

TIP: *Again, 'Menu B' is more effective because it is open to expansion.* That means you can have a variety of sauces for things such as wings, which allows for more menu options while still keeping it simple. The same goes for the flatbreads; different toppings can give more variety. Even the pasta can have different sauces and ingredients. The point in using one category can give you a number of other sub-varieties while still keeping it simple.

Don't throw your menu and food together just to make a quick buck. No one will EVER recommend a basic burger with cheese. The goal is to get a good reputation that gets people talking and customers who return. It starts with quality food, not the price, *and the quality of your food should match your price.*

Don't get me wrong, you are welcome to make up something like 'Menu A' and just throw things together, if you are in it for the quick buck, but for those of you reading who want to build a reputation for a high-quality food truck business, you'll find that the love you put into your food will resonate with your customers, get them talking, and most importantly, they will want to return and eat with you again.

TIP: *Keep an open mind about making changes to your menu, keep an open eye on what items sell best, and consider removing what is not selling.* This allows you to keep your best sellers to make higher sales. Again, keep it simple!

If it's all working, great!

§§§§§

Summary:

- People can taste the love that is put into food so take your time to put the love into your menu.
- What is your truck going to specialize in?
- Your ideas do not have to be unique.
- Use colorful words when describing your menu to give customers a picture in their mind of a mouthwatering experience they will enjoy.
- It's not the people you know, it's the people you don't know who will keep you in business.
- Use quality products and price accordingly.
- People can taste cheap but are also willing to pay for quality items.
- It's about quality, not quantity.
- Work smarter, not harder.
- Keep your menu simple.

Chap III: Do Your Homework

I know you are excited and ready to serve, and that you're ready to have that cash start rolling in!

I'll admit, that was me.

I believe I was meant to make all my mistakes in order to share them with anyone who wants to get their food truck career off the ground and help prevent them from making the same mistakes.

You must do your homework before you jump into this venture. This may seem like a boring step but it's VERY NECESSARY.

What I'm going to tell you can save thousands in cash, hundreds of headaches, and tons of wasted hours. I'm going to give you ideas and strategies that will save money for you in the long run as well. That alone should make this chapter interesting enough.

Scenario:

You and your buddy get drunk one weekend and conceive the notion to weld together a food cart, or maybe you find a food truck for sale from James, who lives up the street. James bought the truck and now wants to sell it because he didn't have the time to get it off the ground, and suddenly, you see your new business come to life right in front of you.

Beware, what appears to be a money maker can be more of a money drainer that puts a dent in your wallet and stops you from getting out and getting started.

Consider checking in with your county Health Department before going into constructing your truck or buying a used rig. Different states and counties have different rules that apply to food vendors. They also have different specifications for the construction of food carts and trucks, plus they will also tell you what type of truck you're going to need for the menu you're planning on serving.

For example, you can't serve seafood from a hot-dog cart. Different size trucks require different types of licenses. Also, a full-size truck license that allows an unlimited variety of food will be more expensive than a taco truck license. Even if you're a professional welder, your county could have a different requirement for a kitchen than you may have anticipated. So, it's best to build according to their requirements from the very beginning.

The same applies to the food truck you want to buy from James, who may have purchased it in a different county or another state, which may need expensive modifications to get it up to code before you can get your food out into the world.

Don't expect to buy or build a food cart or truck the way it is and immediately start serving. **It must pass your county's inspection requirements before that.**

It would be wise to look into those rules before you start construction or purchase a food truck.

Generally, your county health department is more than happy to help you get headed in the right direction. There are food truck builders who can build to your specific county codes, but that can get a bit costly. It's wise to be resourceful, as I will explain further.

TIP: *Keep an eye out for a truck or cart that's for sale and has already been serving food in your county to save you the hassle of finding out your new Frankenstein of a truck won't pass inspection.*

Purchase a truck that is already up to standard because having to modify your truck to fit the specs will cost you a lot of time, hassle, and money, and from having to construct a new truck from scratch.

Inspection costs range from $200.00-$500.00, so make sure you are inspection ready. Although, a new truck may be the only option if the used truck you're considering seems to be falling apart.

Sometimes a new food truck owner can be so passionate about getting started…*me included*, that we buy trucks we shouldn't have. **Don't let your excitement blind you into buying a truck that is falling apart.** An old truck can have maintenance issues from the start. It may be worth it to spend a little extra money on a truck more up-to-date.

Make sure not to go wild with the spending on your new rig, as I will explain soon.

TIP: *Consider purchasing a food trailer that can be hauled instead of a food truck. Why?*

The maintenance on a trailer can be much less than a food truck that you must drive. You can save on engine repair and maintenance by only having your hauling vehicle to maintain. It's the difference between changing four to six tires on a full truck or two for a trailer you can haul, plus, insurance costs can be less, or none at all, because sometimes your car insurance will cover what you're hauling, just make sure your car is covered for commercial use.

Maintenance is going to be inevitable, regardless of what style of rig you have, but I've found that a 'hauling kitchen' will save you more money and troubles throughout your serving time. Just think about it, but ultimately, the choice is up to you.

The price differs in truck sizes. They can range from 5k to 100k. Realize that the smaller you go, the more limited you are in what you can serve. However, I strongly believe you can do as much on a smaller trailer as you can with a large truck.

I don't mean in terms of food storage and space, but in the quality of product and still make a decent living. There is nothing wrong with wanting a large truck for all the reasons given above but you should consider slowly working your way up to a larger truck.

Start small and spend in a way that makes sense.

Something else to keep in mind is if your city or town is not known for having large events, the revenue that you make will not cover the overhead of a larger truck, and vise-versa in bigger cities where there will be many options for large events to reach out to that will help make it easier to reach the revenue you need to maintain a larger rig.

Instead, consider spending on something more in your comfort zone to build your foundation.

Make sure your idea will sell.

Make sure YOU can sell.

Stay motivated for more than a week.

However, if an emergency happens or you find that this sort of life is not for you, you won't find yourself in debt of 100k. Also, keep in mind that just because you got your truck for 100k does not mean that's what you will get for it if you decide to sell it six months later. Do you feel me? You are welcome because I probably just saved you 100k!

However, I do believe you will thrive. The fact that you are reading this book shows that you want to make this happen and you want to succeed.

I'm helping you make the right decisions that will save your bank account and also grow your newfound business from the ground up.

You will grow with your business organically so do it at a pace you're comfortable with.

Trust me when I say, *you'll know when it's time to take the next step.*

It will be organic.

Things don't happen overnight. So, if you're not in it for the long-haul STOP READING NOW.

§§§§§

Summary:

- Do your homework. Don't let your excitement push you into buying a truck that is falling apart.
- Consider working your way up to a larger truck.
- Start small, make your purchase within your budget.
- Before spending big, make sure your idea will sell.
- Make sure YOU can sell and come up with ways to stay motivated enough for more than a week.
- You will grow with your business organically, just allow it to happen at your own pace.

Samantha Ann recommends The Blacktop Grill.
December 14, 2018 ·
Great food and super friendly owner. He was more than happy to explain the menu and offer suggestions for my dietary restrictions. Will definitely be back!
Great food · Creative cuisine · Cheap eats
The Blacktop Grill
1 Comment

Chap IV: Logistics

Working in a food truck is similar to working in a restaurant. Regardless of its size, you are now officially in the customer service industry. You will need a system in place to follow, a system for your weekly tasks, and daily preparation. It does not take rocket science to get a system in place, but your system will definitely help you in running a smoother truck. It will also come in handy when bringing on help or hiring an employee who will need to learn your systems quickly to help make it a smooth-running food truck environment.

For this chapter, I'm assuming you have worked in the restaurant industry before. If not, it won't end your career, but I would recommend taking a part-time job in a restaurant as a busser, server, or host for 6-12 months to experience it firsthand. You might consider a small fast-food restaurant for a part-time job, but no matter the size, you will find that each restaurant has a system in place that helps make it run harmoniously.

You will be able to take away from those systems valuable knowledge to use as your own. Systems that will be vital in helping your own business run smoother.

Another approach can be to reach out to a manager or restaurant owner and offer to do work for free, YES FREE. If allowed, follow along for a week or two and get a feel for how the wheels turn during regular hours. It's priceless knowledge for your sweat equity. The free hours you donate give you PRICELESS information on processes that can be used for your business and give you a clear understanding of how they work.

The easiest approach can be to visit local restaurants and study them from the moment you walk in the door, throughout the meal, and up until the last goodbye.

Keep an eye out for things like:

The feeling you get when you first walk in. Is there a warm greeting? If any at all. What is the interaction like between you the customers and the restaurant staff? What are the processes used by the restaurant from the moment you order until the food is received? Study how the menu looks and the flow of the food items. How was your meal presentation? Was it enticing or not?

TIP: *The McDonald's movie "The Founder," was not only entertaining but also very educational when it comes to systems. If you can, watch it.*

Avoid the dislikes from your experience. Instead, take the likes and incorporate them into your system.

Some things to consider might be:

What would you want a customer to experience if they walked up to your food-truck?

Do you give them a welcoming smile?

Do you speak with confidence about all your items, and happily go over the menu with the customer?

What does your menu look like?

How do you come off to yourself? (*This is a good indicator of how you would come off to a customer.*)

Although your food-truck isn't the same magnitude as a full-service restaurant, getting a part-time job for firsthand experience is the best option to get a feel for the daily tasks, busy hours, common stresses, and allows for a good in-depth glimpse of the restaurant machine, and how it works together as a whole. As a bonus, by getting a job, you will get paid for your work, which you can invest right back into your food-truck.

The daily processes found in a restaurant will be an accurate representation of what your daily duties, tasks, and responsibilities will be like on your rig. More than likely, you will be the one in charge of the day-to-day responsibilities for preparation of the day or week.

In the customer service industry, there is no such thing as a bad day. Meaning, that regardless of what kind of day you have, every interaction you make with a customer must be a positive one, and you should exert the same amount of energy on each person who takes their time to stop in and eat with you.

Some ideas to consider:

Look at your food-truck as a business and a service.

Your job is to help feed people with a smile.

Go into it with a servant's heart.

Become a social butterfly.

You are interacting daily with people…believe me, **they will remember the service they received.**

Make sure to help with questions about the menu.

Don't point a customer's attention to one particular or special item because your whole menu is special.

Know how to cook and be creative.

If you are not, then find someone who is.

Specialize in food that you're good at cooking.

A customer's first bite starts with the eyes.

The presentation of your food gives a preview of what they can expect to come next.

Learn how to work under pressure. (*A food truck is not a good environment if you can't handle stress.*)

Follow up about how the food was, if possible.

Note: This chapter does not cover how to cook or food presentation, I'm assuming you know how to cook or at least have someone who will help you.

§§§§§

Summary:

- When you own a food truck, you are now officially in the customer service industry.
- Get your operating systems in place. This includes both your daily and weekly responsibilities.
- There is no such thing as a bad day in the customer service industry, so smile and make every day a great experience for both you and your customer.

Melissa Kay Hudson reviewed The Blacktop Grill — 5★
September 29, 2016 ·

So good. Amazing service. Happy positive service with amazing food is hard to find.

The Blacktop Grill

Chap V: Your Niche

The rules have long changed from food trucks that sit on corners waiting for customers to come to them. The beauty of a food truck is your ability to go to where the customers are, and not having them come to you.

I often see a new truck that finds a good corner and thinks it's going to be a great "niche," but things don't end up working out as planned. Yet they never tried to do things differently or found new places to serve.

They allow the disappointment to drive them to quit.

I believe the decision to quit most often starts with negative thinking or feeling overwhelmed by it all.

You may have thoughts like, *my food is not good enough, I wasn't meant to do this or I'm never going to get this to where I want to be*. Trust me, we've all had those self-doubts, especially on days when things are just not going our way. These thoughts tend to take a downturn on our motivation. You are going to have slow nights, you are going to have things go wrong, but you will also encounter amazing opportunities, make new friendships, and eventually an income that will make you a living if you just give it a chance to grow.

Even after all my years of service, and the great reputation I've built, I still tend to get those thoughts. I still have slow nights, and I still get events that just don't go the way I anticipated. Try to realize that the good and the bad are all part of the ride.

The trucks that seem to have it all figured out still have the same struggles, but just keep moving forward. They have pushed forward time and time again finding better more efficient ways of doing things.

Everyday work teaches you the dos and don'ts.

This guide cannot cover every detail of what will happen on a daily basis, so you have to put yourself out there and figure things out as your journey continues. Don't allow discouragement over one bad day or one bad event to stop you from moving forward.

You are also a new truck; nobody knows about your great food just yet. Part of your job is to organically change that by going out on the street every day and to consistently let the world know you exist.

You will find many places to consider where you can serve that will allow you to grow your reputation one day at a time as well as your take-home income.

Get your food noticed faster by changing up your stops and choosing different areas around your town or in your city. Once I've found the niches that seem to work best for me, I don't veer too far from them unless the opportunity appears to be a good one. Trust me, once the ball starts rolling, there will be no lack of work.

Before too long your phone won't stop ringing with constant calls for you to cater events or parties.

Another thing to consider is whether you're going to be a full-time or a part-time truck. If you want to be a weekend warrior, that's fine, but be sure to work enough events to cover the yearly licensing and permits to keep your business open legally and still put some money in your pocket. If you're in it full-time, like me, you need a steady flow of work. Don't quit your day job just yet, let your food truck ease you out of the job by replacing those job hours with days you work on your rig.

There are many options around your town that you may not have considered, which I will list below.

They work best for me and are worth considering, so you might want to try them all. As time progresses, focus on the stops that you find most feasible but most importantly that you enjoy the most to work at.

The more options you have, the more opportunities. Trust me when I say, *there is no lack of opportunities.*

Bars and Breweries:

These can be a good source of income and consistent stops in your schedule because of the people looking for a bite to eat and a cold drink after a hard day's work.

Check out places that have no kitchen and those that do not serve food. You'll be amazed by all the 'yeses' they give you to park out front and serve your meals.

A bar with no food means the patrons have to go elsewhere to eat, and having your truck there keeps their customers drinking longer, so bar and brewery owners love this. I recommend trying bigger, more popular bars or breweries because they'll have more space for more people. The more mouths you can feed, the better the take-home income. Also, consider working on karaoke, trivia, or spelling bee night, etc., it will only take a few hours to make a quick buck on busy nights like these.

Food Truck Round-Ups:

A food truck round-up is a large gathering of food trucks and vendors that serve different parts of the city on a weekly or monthly basis. See how to get involved.

These tend to have a few more food options, and with it, competition, but if your food is exciting you will get attention away from the basic food vendors.

You can find local groups like these on Facebook.

Large Events:

Concerts and larger events like the County Fair may charge a large fee to attend, but the amount of food you will serve may make the time and money worth it.

Keep your catering options open: Lunch-ins, dinner parties, and weddings are all great sources of income. Make sure you have business cards at hand and make it visible and vocal that you cater.

TIP: *Call around and get an idea of what restaurants charge for food similar to yours for catering.*

Price your services below or near their prices for a competitive advantage, then use that to your advantage by mentioning to your potential customers how much they will be saving when buying from you.

Food Truck Groups on Facebook:

On Facebook, people reach out to these groups that are in need of food vendors for their events.

Local Swap Meet(s):

Swap Meets are known not only for a good deal but also for good food. These are worth looking into.

They may require a daily rent but the foot traffic you find there is maybe worth the try.

Farmers Markets:

People go there for fresh groceries, but you can also find foodies that are on the lookout for exciting eats like yours. These markets may charge small fees, but you can guarantee that you will find people ready to eat.

Local University or Community College:

It may work better for you than it did for me, but a couple of things to keep in mind are that these places may try to charge you a large fee to serve on campus.

You may also have some difficulty finding a parking space because campuses tend to charge for just about everything, including parking. If there is an open corner or lot where you can set up near the school's property that you think will get traffic, then it's worth the try.

Office Buildings:

Keep an eye out for office buildings with a lack of food options in their surrounding area. Office workers only get an hour for lunch, if they are lucky, and need a nearby food outlet. Speak to some of the offices in the complex for feedback about setting up your rig.

Consider every other week so that people don't get tired of your food or bored with you being there.

You can set up a schedule at different commercial centers to fill in your days. Keep switching your stops until you find which places work best for you.

At the end of the day, it is totally up to you to make a schedule that best suits your particular needs.

Start slowly with maybe one event every weekend. This will give you a chance to get a feel for your new rig and other obstacles you might experience. Practice serving and cooking quickly, especially if you have no prior experience doing so. Make sure you ask customers for feedback about your food and make adjustments where necessary. Also, get comfortable with the day's requirements for your rig to make it a much smoother experience when you're out serving.

You are now your own boss and must find ways to keep yourself motivated. To see a steady income, you need to be consistent in your days out and selling food. Keeping it consistent doesn't guarantee you will make a huge buck every time out but will instill a good habit of working your rig regardless of your projected outcome.

I've had nights that started slowly and ended great. Nights that were supposed to be slow because of a game or a fight, but I still ended up making good money.

My realization was that not everyone is into sports. I also don't get discouraged by a rainy day. People still want to eat at my routine stops regardless of the weather. *(Except in Kansas…stay home if you see a tornado!)*

I've also found that on the days my mind and body just don't feel like working are often the days I make the most money. It's a weird coincidence, but it happens all the time, so I follow through on those days.

TIP: *Start a Facebook and Instagram page for your business and keep them updated.* Start by filling out the information about you and your food truck. Make sure to add pleasing pictures of your food and your truck.

Use social media regularly, as I will discuss later.

Starting social media accounts will get you traffic. These platforms will also let people know you exist and of your whereabouts. Use the “Create an Event” option on your Facebook page as a tool to show where and when your stops are scheduled. This will allow you to invite your friends to follow where you will be serving.

This also allows people to find your whereabouts and visit your truck. If people are curious about your food, you can easily refer them to your events page to find the stop most convenient for them.

§§§§§

Summary

- The beauty of a food truck is its mobility.
- The good and the bad are all part of the ride.
- Everyday work teaches you the dos and don’ts.
- Don’t let one bad day or event stop you.
- Ease out of your day job slowly. The days you work on your rig will eventually replace those job hours.
- Maintain the stops that you find most feasible, but more importantly, that you enjoy working at.
- Consistency in the way you function is mandatory if you want to see a steady income on your days out.

Joseph Gauci recommends The Blacktop Grill.
Jan 4 at 7:30 PM
Fantastic food. Very fast service! This is the kind of trailer that you plan your evenings around!
Great food

Chap VI: A Little Extra Income Helps

Small business owners can now make money more easily because there is so much technology available to them to take advantage of extra streams of income.

It's no longer a cash-only world but cash is still king.

When I was first starting, I wasn't aware that these options were so easily accessible. I knew they existed but just assumed they were very complicated to learn and were an expensive process to purchase and use.

In the beginning, I only accepted cash, but I quickly discovered that many of my first-time customers only carried credit or debit cards, and realized just how much income I was going to miss out on if I didn't learn to take advantage of these revenue streams.

Throughout my years of serving, I found the options listed below to work the best for me, so I encourage you to take advantage of any or all of them.

Cash:

Accept it, love it, and roll in it… cash is king.

Card Readers:

There are many companies out there that will try and convince you that their card reader is the best choice for you by offering a smaller fee per transaction, however, I've found their hardware to be really expensive.

If the hardware gets lost or stolen, it can be tough on the wallet, and it can also be a pain having to request and wait for a replacement. I found that Square Reader is by far the best choice. Square Reader charges a small fee that they take from each transaction, but it is well worth the easy setup, and the hardware is inexpensive.

You can find the most basic Square Reader at any Walmart, Walgreens, or Office Depot to buy or replace for only $10.00, which you can use with their app right from your phone. Square also has other options for card readers that can be a little pricier, depending on the kind of device you choose, but the $10.00 mobile reader has been my go-to since day one.

Square also keeps your sales records online to give you a view of your daily, monthly, or yearly reports, which are easy to read, and what reports should be.

Note: I am not a representative, nor am I associated with any company I recommend is this book. These are only companies I have used when I was starting and now recommend for your own start-up.

Since this publishing, “Tap to Pay” is now on your cell phone through Square as well, making it even easier for customers to just tap their credit or debit card on your cell phone to send payments.

I once tried changing to a company that offered less of a fee but found they were charging other hidden fees that I could not keep track of. The reports they would send were large and tedious. Transactions should be simple and not complicated in any area of business.

In my opinion, Square fills all the check marks.

It is easy to understand, has no hidden fees, it’s easy to start up and has inexpensive equipment. I personally do not mind paying for any reasonable fee if a service or company saves me time and makes my life easier.

On your Square dashboard, make sure to set yourself up to accept tips but also set up state, and county taxes.

Take advantage of the tax options so that you don’t have to pay out of pocket at the end of the year.

The sales tax option adds the current tax to each sale at checkout for customers to pay. That way, you're not stuck with a large tax bill at the end of the month…and don't forget to activate the tipping option as well.

Also, make sure you place a jar out for cash tips at your workstation for people to see… a little extra adds up. I found that tips alone, between my jar and swipes, make me $30-$80 a night on average.

Ready, drum roll… that's an extra $9,000 a year!

Catering Events:

Take advantage of all catering opportunities.

Large events, business events, and private parties

Look into pricing from similar catering companies or restaurants and be competitive with their prices.

It will save you the time of having to figure out prices on your own and underpricing your services.

TIP: *Let customers know that you happily accept gratuities and place a tip jar out during these events.*

I've earned tips as high as $400.00 from the party planners but also the people who are eating tend to tip more when they are not paying for their meal.

Food Carriers:

In every city, there are many different food carriers or delivery platforms currently available for food trucks to take advantage of.

The carriers I use are:

Uber Eats.

Door Dash

Grubhub.

Postmates.

They average a 30% commission per order.

Example: (If you get an order for $50.00, the carrier will get $15.00. This might seem high but I'm happy to pay for what they offer in return.

TIP: *Add a reasonable amount to your online menu prices to help cover the cost of some of these platforms' commissions, which you do from your dashboard.*

I also added 'call ahead ordering' as an option for customers to pick up and found it to be a fruitful move.

The benefit you will get from most of these carriers is marketing on their websites to customers who may not normally know what you are serving.

Having your food truck visible to your customers over a 5 to 10-mile radius saves you time from having to deliver the food yourself and provides an excellent extra source of new income.

It also lets the public know you exist, which gives you the potential for getting a new returning customer.

Most of these platforms offer a free start-up just for signing up with them, and as a bonus, some send out a professional photographer to take pictures of your food.

I recommend you take the time to get a professional photographer of your own to take eye-pleasing photos of your food and use them on your personal pages.

If you are serving different areas of town, you can update your address for each stop on the merchant sites.

Each of these carriers has a tablet they will send you, but managing all of the updates can be a little hard to maintain, so I use a company called "Try Otter," which manages all your platforms from one device.

They charge $15.00 a month for their service but it has been a great experience to have my orders directed to one place, and the customer service is amazing.

(Note) Since the writing of this book, the prices for "Try Otter" services may have changed

You can take advantage of Otter's customer service straight from the tablet through their chat box, or by email for quick replies. If any changes need to be made to any or all of my platforms, they are quick to help. You can also make changes from your "Otter" dashboard and also update all your other platforms simultaneously.

I can serve different areas daily and can update my address with Otter to wherever my destination I'm at, or I can open up right in my neighborhood for delivery.

I average 3 to 5 orders a day from these platforms, which quickly adds up. Every little bit helps.

If you have a great corner in a heavily populated area like downtown or a large neighborhood, you may find these carriers get you extra orders for extra income.

TIP: *If you don't have Wi-Fi access, which you must have for most of these carriers, I've discovered that through my phone's service, Hotspot was only $10.00 extra a month, which allows me to use my cell phone as Wi-Fi from anywhere that service is available.*

There are many options to make an extra dollar.

I constantly preach simplicity.

I keep my business simple and let the options above make me the extra dollars.

You can choose to make extra money in different ways like serving chips, popcorn, and other fillers, but I've found that keeping up with so many options can be tough and also not worth such a small amount of money for all the hassle. I prefer big dollars, so I always focus on the higher-priced items on my menu.

§§§§

Summary:

- It's no longer a cash-only world, but cash is king.
- Transactions should be simple and not complicated in any area of your business.
- Don't fret about fees, especially if a platform takes work off your plate and makes you additional income.
- Accept tips on your card reader but also have a tip jar in plain sight on your truck. You will find that the tips add up significantly each year.
- Always remember to keep things simple.

Chap VII: Time Management

Time management is needed to avoid overwhelm. Yes, a food truck business can be a bit overwhelming,

I've given you a lot to think about and consider. Even when you finally find yourself on the road and are ready to serve the stress doesn't seem to end, you may accidentally forget to fill your propane tanks and run out while you're in the middle of serving. Even getting to your destination can be a challenge because you may be running late due to traffic. Maybe you have to stop at multiple grocery stores for crucial ingredients, or your mind is racing, trying to cover all the daily details, and you haven't even started serving yet! These are just a few examples of everyday stresses of a food truck life.

Stop, take a breath, take a moment to pat yourself on the back because you're making it happen, you're making moves, you're making progress!

Starting a new venture is a lot like getting started at a new job. When first starting out you have no idea what you are doing and processing all the new information as best you can. *You learn as you go. You learn and grow.* As you go it gets easier, it becomes second nature, but it's normal to feel overwhelmed while in the process, especially as a new food truck owner. You're doing something new, veering off the beaten path. Try not to overstress when you make a mistake or come across a problem. These stresses are going to help you adjust and before you know it, all this will soon be second nature, kind of like a new job. Throw yourself out there.

Make mistakes. It's ok!

After many hard lessons and stresses, I figured out better and more efficient ways of doing things. I also figured out that a lot of my stress and overwhelm were caused by mismanagement of my time, which also had a significant effect on my mental space. Let me explain.

Starting out, I still had an "employee mentality" from so many years of having worked for someone else. Meaning, that when you have a job there is a set time that you must be ready and working by, say 8:00 a.m., so when you are running late, you start feeling anxious and rush to get there on time, right?

When becoming your own boss, you're going to feel the same anxiety to get out on the road, set up, and start serving. It's almost as if someone is watching over you. Get that out of your head. You no longer have someone hovering over you, pushing you, or demanding that you get your tasks accomplished. The responsibility is now all yours. If you're running a little late, no one cares.

However, I do recommend that you always try your best to get to your destination on time.

Your goal is to have your prep, truck, and yourself ready at a pace you can handle. Spread out every task into daily chores throughout the week.

Implementing this idea alone will save you TONS of energy and headaches. You are allowed only so much mind and body energy per day and strategies like these will give you extra energy from any unnecessary stress. Extra energy that will help get you through your day.

Sometimes events such as a catering gig may have a specific time they want you to show up, so be sure to use your time wisely by prepping yourself and your rig far ahead of time to get to these events with ease. If you mess up they probably won't ask you back again.

It was always a bit of a challenge for me to prepare for the average day, get out the door, and make it to my destination on time because I was overstuffing my day to the point of mental and physical exhaustion.

I found that simply making a couple of shifts in my daily time management made a huge difference.

For example, if I had an event, I would stuff the shopping and prepping into the same day of the event then still try to go out with a smile on my face, serve food, and finally clean up and then get ready to do it all over again the very next day. I was exhausted after each workday and dreaded the following day knowing the same exhausting work was waiting for me.

My mistake was trying to keep my days off as days off and keep my workdays for work, but when I learned to incorporate my work with my personal life and had a system in place that spread my daily tasks throughout the week, it all became much more manageable.

Self-motivation also plays a major role in this line of work. Realize, your preparation is not being paid for. What you're getting paid for is the outcome and reward for all that preparation and hard work.

Proper preparation allows your serving hours to move smoothly and make the smoothest dollar possible.

Then you'll be done and on your way to the bank.

Most importantly, like myself, you're not setting yourself up to be overwhelmed and over-fatigued.

Study your schedule for the week and spread out your responsibilities to help set yourself up for success.

Why weekly? You may ask.

I find that prepping weekly allows my food to be at its freshest, also keep in mind that prepping never ends. It's constant refilling of your items. I buy what's on my prep list every week for maximum freshness and find that I have less wasted food by doing so.

Here is what my average week consists of:

Monday	Make a shopping list.
	Buy what's on the list.
	What is your cart or truck in need of?
Tuesday	Prep your cart or truck.
	Prep the Food
Wednesday	Serve from 5 pm to 9 pm
Thursday	Serve from 5 pm to 9 pm
Friday	Serve from 5 pm to 9 pm

Saturday Serve from 5 pm to 9 pm

Sunday Serve from 12 pm to 6 pm

Your week may look slightly different depending on what days you are serving, but this will help you better understand the importance of spreading out your tasks. Each task normally takes 1 to 2 hours, which can add up, especially if you try and stuff them into one day.

Expect to work seven days a week. As any business owner will tell you, *their business is their life*. You must learn to incorporate your business into your life.

However, for weekend warriors, your schedule will differ, but time management is still critical even if you have a full-time job. You must be in it for the long haul. STOP READING NOW if you're not fully committed.

After looking at my schedule above you may have asked yourself, *how was I able to make a buck working only four hours?* Here are some serving facts that will give you strategic times to be set up and when to serve.

Over my twenty years of being in the food industry, these are known times and days when people eat …

Breakfast 6 am to 10 am

Lunch 11 am to 2 pm

Dinner 5 pm to 9 pm

Late-night 10 pm to 3 am

Monday, Tuesday, and Wednesday tend to be a little slower unless you can find some fruitful events to serve.

Thursday, Friday, Saturday, and Sunday are when people start hitting the town for food and drinks.

The majority of my time goes to preparation.

The minimum of my time goes to serving the food.

My day tends to be longer if I am hired to do a lunch gig or another event. My usual four hours also fluctuate depending on how slow the night is. You may want to cut your losses and close up earlier if that's the case. You must learn to read the crowd and decide when there is no more traffic and move on.

I take advantage of the times when people will most likely be eating. No more, no less. I try to make as much as I can in those time frames and move on with my day, but I don't wait around hoping for business. You don't want to be sitting around wasting your valuable time.

Although, even If I think it will be slow, I make it a point to stay at least three hours. There have been many nights where it has been slow for the first two hours, and suddenly customers start rolling in and it ends up being a good night after all. However, sometimes it's reversed.

It could be busy for the first two hours then die out. There's just no way to predict this so make it a habit to stay a set amount of time before packing up for the day.

TIP: *Costco and Walmart (depending on your area) now offer delivery.* Both stores charge a fee or tack on extra to the prices, but I find it is well worth the time and energy I save from having to go to these stores many times a week especially if my schedule is overloaded. Also, Walmart now has pick-up options, so that you can order ahead and just swing by at the available time slot. Take advantage of these. Remember, we only have so much energy and brain space to use daily. Use it wisely.

§§§§§

Summary:

- Study your week.
- Spread out all of your tasks into daily chores that you do throughout the week.
- Realize that your preparation is not being paid for, rather, you're getting paid for the outcome of that preparation.

- Factor in time for your drive and set up.
- This gig is seven days a week.
- Incorporate your business into your life.
- Take advantage of the times when people will most likely be eating breakfast, lunch, and dinner.
- There are no more bosses to get on you if you're late.
- The responsibility is now all yours.
- Remember we only have so much energy and brain space to use each day. Use yours wisely.

Michael Lazaro recommends The Blacktop Grill.
January 17, 2019 ·
Amazing Food Truck that everyone visiting Tucson AZ should try
Creative cuisine · Great food · Cheap eats
The Blacktop Grill
1 Comment

Chap VIII: Facing Challenges

As I was coming to the end of my first year in the food truck business I was still figuring a few things out, but I had a good grasp on it and just needed to keep a steady workflow going. Around that time, I was invited to be a vendor for a huge soccer tournament hosted by the city at public parks all around town. The soccer field I was invited to be a vendor at was one of the bigger parks in the city which was estimated to have more than 10,000 people visit that weekend for the tournaments.

This was going to be my ticket to the big buck.

There would be other vendors as well but with an expectancy of 10,000 people, there should be plenty of sunshine for everyone. Prior to the event, I spent every day for two weeks prepping for this big tournament.

I went all out with printed t-shirts, new ice chests to hold my prep, and a team consisting of my wife and two brothers who I couldn't wait to pay top dollar too for helping me serve at such an epic event.

I prepped eight times the amount of product I would normally carry spending right around $2000.00 in total but expecting to make eight times that after this epic weekend … but I was headed for a rude awakening.

The Parks and Recreation Department did not only invite local vendors but also corporate vendors such as McDonalds and Pizza Hut, which small businesses just can't compete with due to their marketing budget.

We were placed right next to a 20-foot-tall balloon of Ronald McDonald and a business-savvy Pizza Hut that was making freshly baked pizzas on the spot.

To top it off, our location in the park was where the children's tournament was held. Every kid was flocking straight to the oversized Ronald McDonald and pizzas.

I quickly discovered that just because 10,000 people are expected to attend an event doesn't mean all of them are going to eat … it was mind-blowing.

We ended up only making a fraction of the expenses back, which wasn't worth the heartbreak or preparation of such a huge failure. I was devastated and got stuck with piles … and I mean piles, of over-prep.

I wouldn't change that experience for the world.

That nightmare weekend has saved me from the same mistake many times over. Every day holds its fair share of challenges. Some are more challenging than others, but that's part of life. Don't be discouraged by the challenges that lie ahead, face them.

Even your regular 9 to 5 job has its daily challenges and overly stressful days. In this case, you must face the challenges involved with owning your own food truck business. No one is exempt, not you or me.

Learn to accept it, *things are going to go wrong.*

Some days will SUCK but it's how you respond to those mistakes that allows you to learn and move on.

I doubt that the challenges you face will be quite as epic as my run-in with a giant-size Ronald McDonald but sharing that experience should save you from the task of over-prepping for future events yourself.

As for food prepping for large events now, I prep only double the amount of my average busy night. Meaning, I prep what it would take to sell out on a busy night and double that. If I sell it all, great! I walk home with a great profit that I'm more than happy with.

If I don't sell it all, I can quickly recover and sell the extra another day. This strategy also allows me not to be stuck with excess prep that I do not have the storage space to handle. As a bonus, this is also a money and time saver. You will know what that prep looks like for you soon enough. Once you figure that out, double it for large events. This strategy will save you every time.

Here are a few other challenges you might come across during the everyday grind.

The Man

It seems simple enough … buy a truck, make good food, park, and sell the food … but you can always be sure "The Man" wants their cut. Each city, county, and state has its own set of regulations for food trucks that require you as the owner to obtain several permits and certifications, otherwise, you can be fined.

Some of these permits include:

1. City Business License
2. Health Department Certification
3. Food Safety Training
4. Permits and licenses for the truck itself, such as registration, inspection, driver's license, etc.

5. Liability Insurance
6. Peddlers License (in certain suburbs, your city may require that you have one)
7. Event Fees
8. Paying taxes

§§§§§

TIP: *For the best-priced insurance for a food truck, and also the best coverage, try flipogram.com (FLIP), which runs about $300.00 a year.*

You must pay the premium upfront, but it's better than using your personal use auto insurance company, which can be double or triple the amount.

If you are hauling a food trailer, inquire with your auto insurance company to see if trailers are covered or if adding it to your coverage is even possible.

Note: Since the writing of this book, I found that my full coverage vehicle insurance covered my food trailer. Make sure that you speak with your insurance provider to compare what coverages are available.

Do your homework.

Compare prices.

Go with what works best.

Facilities:

In some cities, food trucks are limited by available toilet facilities. For example, in some major cities, if a food truck is parked in one location for longer than an hour, there must be a bathroom facility within 500 feet.

Other cities have similar regulations that become a challenge for food trucks. This rule has recently been applied in my city, but all my stops have restrooms that are close and available. Larger events that you're invited to attend will always provide these facilities.

Parking

You can't always park wherever you want.

Some food trucks must lease their spots ahead of time or have deals set up with business owners.

Other spots require a percentage of your sales.

Many times there are waiting lists for parking spots at lunch spots, fairs, farmers' markets, and other events.

Parking is often more than simply finding an open parking lot and setting up a shop, especially if you want a spot in the highest traffic areas.

Feel out your areas.

Choose your best stops, and work those.

Prep

Food trucks are built with food preparation in mind, but not so when it comes to food storage, so buying in bulk is not a good idea.

Shuttling food from a store to your truck is almost a daily occurrence. You might argue that it's more efficient to take the food truck to the supermarket until you realize that some trucks only get seven miles per gallon of gas. You might consider strategizing your stops if they are on the way to your serving destination.

Keep in mind that Costco and Walmart now deliver.

Weather

You can control your food quality and how you run your business, but you can't control the weather.

Depending on where you live, the weather may be a factor, or not. Rain or shine, I go out to my regular stops and still make a buck. You have to judge for yourself how the elements in your area will affect your business.

Jack of all Trades

It's not enough to properly maintain your cooking equipment. You must also make your truck runs reliable enough to get you to your scheduled events. All trucks require regular maintenance, repairs, gas, and new tires.

The more you learn about how to make automotive repairs, the better off you'll be. These days, I delegate most of the time-consuming maintenance. If it's a small project that I can accomplish in a couple of hours, I'll do the work myself to save money but don't be afraid to delegate big tasks to take pressure off your plate.

TIP: *Find a mobile mechanic/welder and keep their contacts in your phone.* They can save you headaches and are well worth the money in case you need a large project done professionally for you.

Consider full coverage insurance for your vehicle/s. Most full coverage insurance includes free towing that can be used in the event of a breakdown.

Staff

A full-time employee may be out of the question to begin but you can find trustworthy help, someone who is looking for an extra buck or just looking for the fun experience of working a food truck.

You can also ask family or friends.

I find that I can handle the basic day-to-day work all by myself, but if I know I have an extra busy stop or large event, I have people who I reach out to for help.

Busy weeks

Depending on how hard you want to go, you can fill your schedule with as many stops as you like.

Even when you get a consistent route, you will still be contacted now and then for unexpected events.

It will happen naturally, so depending on how much you want to take on is entirely your choice.

Making all that good money can be very taxing, so I usually don't consider an event if I don't think it fits me or if someone tries to create a last-minute schedule. I've found that the extra stress and strain are usually not worth it, but of course, the decision is yours to make.

Impatient People

They exist, so exercise patience. A strategy that I use when someone is unpleasant is to make their order first and get them out of the way quickly, regardless of their place in line … just to save my mood.

§§§§§

Summary:

- Just because 10,000 people are expected to attend doesn't mean all of them are going to eat. I recommend you prep double on your average busy nights for large events. If you sell out, great! And if you don't, you can still salvage and resell the extra prep another day.
- Each day will hold its fair share of challenges.
- No one is exempt from challenges, not you or me.
- A nightmare situation can save you from making the same mistake again many times over.

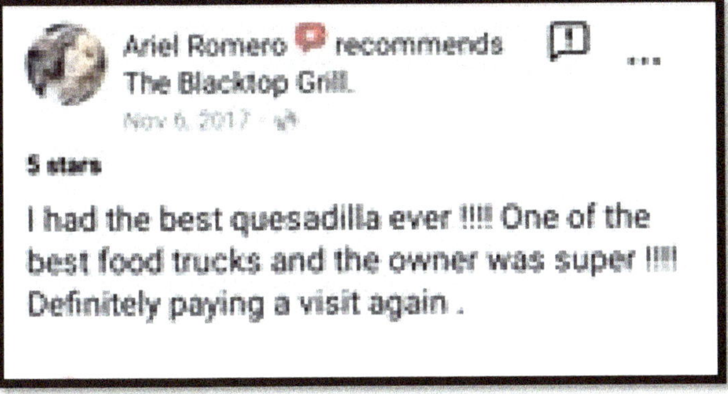

Maritza Torres recommends The Blacktop Grill.

Feb 23, 2018 ·

5 stars

Highly recommend trying this. The food was interestingly finger lickin' good!! I had my doubts at first... I was like quesadilla and hot dogs?!? No thank you... but believe me.. you'll wanna try this place, it's not your average tortilla with cheese or your average hot dog. This place has it's special zing �

Chap IX: Social Media & Marketing

There was a time when TV, radio, and billboards ruled the world as the main streams of promotion for businesses to create awareness and show their products to the world. Today, companies pay massive amounts of money for a 15-second commercial…and social media has taken over the larger networks, meaning that more people are now on social media than television. Why?

Consumers watch what they want, where they want, which is bad for large networks but good for you. Why?

With more people on social media, you now have endless ways to make your own mini-commercial and it's easier to promote your name and your product to the public through all of the various social media sites.

It's faster, and best of all, it's for free.

You also have the option of paying a small fee to boost your post to reach a much larger audience.

I'll talk about that soon, but the boost option only costs pennies as opposed to other forms of advertising.

There are many social media sites available to you today that you should take the time to learn how to use and take full advantage of as a new business owner.

I won't list all the social media platforms here, just a couple as an example. I encourage you to use as many as you can whether or not you like social media because it's a vital step that gets your food and business noticed quickly, plus it's a faster way to connect with customers and let the world know about your business.

People can search for your business straight through social media with a click of a button. This also allows potential customers to contact you without the need for a phone call through these platforms.

Open an account for your business on each of the platforms you choose. Take time to teach yourself to use each platform as best you can. Your page doesn't have to be at peak performance overnight or even have many followers right away, but make sure that you post new content often, be consistent, work on them daily, and get your sight looking as professional as possible. The rest will come organically as time goes on. It only takes about ten minutes a day to add photos, updates, and take away or adjust content or information. Think of these platforms as your own personal store. What would you want a customer to see when they walk into your store?

The most common mistake that I will share with you about social media is constantly seeing business owners use their platforms as personal platforms rather than just doing business. I beg you, PLEASE leave your personal life, beliefs, complaints, opinions, religion, and politics out of it. Keep it strictly about business, otherwise, it's the quickest way to lose present or future customers. Business platforms should always be neutral ground.

Please also note that as a business owner, even your personal pages should reflect your business, so I advise you to keep it neutral as well. Instead, take the time to share your new business page with friends, share your new menu, and share your business wherever possible. Spread the word and make a habit to do it consistently.

'Facebook' is the giant social media site everyone is a part of, so you want to be a part of it too. Facebook allows you to start a business page for free that can be used as a personal website to reach potential customers by letting people know what you're about.

Take your time to properly fill in the info about your business because whether you know it or not, people are always scrolling through social media sites. Make sure your site is up-to-date and as professional as possible.

Take your time to make your site stand out with great-looking photographs. Start with some photos of your food and give descriptions, also photos of your truck, and maybe a photo or video of yourself telling people about your passion for food or of your mission.

People resonate with an individual and his story.

'Boost' is a Facebook option you can take advantage of when you are excited about a new item or have an event that you want to share. This option allows you to reach a larger audience for a small fee that can be easily adjusted to fit your budget. Use this option as often as you can in order to share a new or existing menu item. Take time to describe your item using descriptive words that will grab a viewer's attention. A good picture and a mouth-watering description of food will engage more people and get them curious about your truck.

'Create an Event' is a Facebook option that allows you to create an event that you can invite people to join.

Note: the events you create can also be boosted.

I personally use the 'Events' option as a calendar for my monthly stops. I update my events every month, which shows the locations and times I will be serving throughout the month. I refer people to my events page so they can always know my whereabouts.

I normally try to book my stops one or two months in advance, so I make sure to have all that information updated before the start of every month.

As a new food vendor, it may take time to build a full month's worth of events, but when you get a gig, you can take advantage of creating an event so that you can invite your friends and family. This will get you free publicity and people will be curious to come out and try.

Facebook can also be utilized the same as a webpage for referring people. Don't be discouraged by the likes your page does not get at your start-up stage. It's a waste of your time trying to get likes for your page. It's best to start by working on your page so that it looks good and as professional as possible. People will engage with your page organically. It's your responsibility to make it eye-catching to keep the engagement of customers.

The likes your page gets will also come organically if you're putting the proper amount of energy into your social media. Use Facebook as a tool to quickly spread your truck's name to those who don't know you exist.

The only negative feature of a Facebook business page is that it limits who sees your posts.

This is Facebook's way to make money by offering the business owner the 'Boost' option after every post. My advice is to use the Boost option as often as you can. You don't need to do it for every post but take advantage of Boost when you're showing off a new item on your menu. Keep the posting consistent. People are always on social media. Though Facebook limits your posts, when people do refer to your page, they will see great photos and descriptions waiting for them that will draw them in and want to give your food a try. This will also slowly build the following of people you're looking for.

'Instagram' is my personal favorite because not only does it allow you to create a page for your business, but it focuses more on photographs that allow you to add descriptions and knowledge-sharing along with them. Plus, it is also free and is used by millions of businesses.

If you're not familiar with Instagram, it's worth the know-how to reach people in your city as well as those from afar. I use it not only to show off my food but for inspiration as well. There are many other restaurants, food trucks, and vendors that display edible works of art that I look to for ideas, ingredients, and presentations.

I won't get into grand detail here about how to use Instagram, but I will give you some small pointers and emphasize how important it is to take advantage of it.

I recommend looking for detailed tutorials on uses and practices on YouTube, but the most important thing is taking your time to take great-looking pictures.

Refer to other sights to see the angles and lighting they use to capture a great photo of food. You don't need to be an expert photographer to take a great photo, but if you don't trust your picture-taking skills then consider getting a friend to do it for you or hire a professional.

You must use high-quality photos that will capture people's attention, and you want everything on your site to look professional. You will feel much better if your site appears to be as professionally made as possible.

You may be wondering how to keep social media content fresh when you only have a limited menu.

Take a photograph of a single menu item or multiple items but use several angles to create new images.

Take photos of ingredients like fresh-cut tomatoes, or grilled onions. Showing pictures of your menu's fresh ingredients is a good strategy for capturing attention.

Here are some things to show in your photos:

- An item you just experimented with.
- You and your staff.
- Various angles of your truck.
- Your events.
- Smiling customers eating your food.
- Your new merchandise.

If you keep it fun and creative, that will keep it fresh for you, your content, and your future customers.

Like Facebook, millions of people will flock to see what's new on Instagram daily. Your pictures are going to tell your story and grab the attention of a passerby.

A mistake I was making early on was using memes to fill in the photos, which is fine to do occasionally, but your page can end up becoming a comedy club instead of the importance of your food and your brand.

Focus more on your food and less on the memes.

I was overusing memes because I was running out of ideas for photos. The ultimate goal is to show off your food by using as many photos of it as you can, so to correct this, I found new creative ways to take photos, although an occasional meme is still fun.

It's also okay to recycle a picture but just make sure you use it at a later date so that your pictures don't seem redundant. Have a photo shoot and have fun with it.

The list goes on and on, but this should give you some idea of how to think about your photos.

Once your path to food glory has started, people will leave comments about your food on your posts.

Stay engaged with the public as much as you can by commenting back and keeping communication alive.

This allows people to feel like there is an open door with you to communicate and ask questions.

Start building the relationship with your customers both in person and on social media.

TIP: *Your Facebook business page and Instagram page can be connected so that the pictures you share on one will automatically be posted to the other.* Doing this will save you a lot of time by not having to jump from one platform to another. This works for Twitter as well should you decide to add it to your social media arsenal.

'Yelp' is another great platform for an account.

Customers use it to find local eateries in their area. People can leave a review about their experience after visiting a restaurant, which includes food trucks.

I recommend starting a Yelp account. Not only is it free but it's also a platform that refers people to you.

Now that you're in the customer service industry, you want everyone to have a great experience when they visit your food truck. Yelp reviews can attract customers to you but can also repel them. Like friends, family, and customers, Yelp can be your online word of mouth but does it for a much larger audience.

Like on other platforms, always use great-looking photos to attract people, giving them a good description of what your truck is about. As your business grows, Yelp users will be posting photos and reviews for others to see, so please understand my emphasis on the power of the smile, great food, and presentation.

TIP: *Be prepared to receive phone calls from a Yelp marketer to upgrade to a monthly subscription account.* The upgraded accounts do give you a further reach for customers but can run up to $200 monthly.

Yes, I do think it works. Yes, I know it can reach a further audience, but when you are first starting, use the free platforms until you grow. Later, you may choose to purchase an upgraded account if it fits into your budget.

Having a website created can be expensive to start, however, when you can, you should consider doing so.

Note: Many different sites provide a free webpage.

I prefer 'Wix.' I find it easy to use and also have fun being creative by making sure my website looks the way I want. It's an easy step-by-step process that allows you to save your work as you go, and you can use it for free. At any time, you can purchase your own domain name, which will cost a low monthly fee, but in the meantime, you can take advantage of the free services Wix offers.

'Fiverr' can also be used to help grow your business. I discovered Fiverr while writing this book. You can find inexpensive freelancers from almost any field you may need through Fiverr. When building a business, you must do a lot more with less. Your focus should be on growing your business, which can be a lot to manage. You can make it easier on yourself by delegating certain projects to freelancers who will happily take the work off your plate. With Fiverr, you don't have to go through the hassle of contracts or negotiations, and it also takes away the risk of working with the wrong freelancer.

Fiverr has different price options that will allow you to stay in your budget. It has reviews for each freelancer along with previews of their work that allow for easier decision-making on your end on who to choose. Don't be afraid to delegate if it takes pressure off your plate.

TIP: *Find a freelancer to design or update your logo and website.* This makes your business look more professional, which is important.

§§§§§

Summary:

- Whether you like social media or not, this is a vital step to getting your food and business noticed faster.
- Leave your personal and religious beliefs, politics, complaints, opinions, and stories about your life off of your business pages. Doing this can quickly repel people from your business.
- Your personal page also reflects your business.
- People resonate with stories about your business.
- Your pictures are the best way to tell your story and grab the attention of a passerby.
- Don't waste your time fighting for 'likes' for your business page. Instead, focus on building your sites.
- Your followers will come organically.
- Refer to other sites for ideas to use as your own.
- Start building a personal relationship with your customers, both in person and on social media.
- Yelp reviews can attract people or repel them.

- Understand the power of smiling, great food, and presentation.
- Don't be afraid to delegate work to freelancers to take pressure off your shoulders.
- It's worth it in the long run to avoid becoming too stressed out.

Chap X: Your Finances (Take Control)

For the record, I am not a financial advisor, but I find that your finances can play an important role when jumping into this food truck business, both as a start-up and during your serving career.

I won't get too deep into the subject of finances, but in my opinion, the first steps you should be taking are getting your menu in place (as explained in Chapter 2) and taking control of your finances. If your menu is done and you have control of your money, great! If not, you already know the debts that are poking at your back and need your attention. Is taking on the start-up cost of a food truck going to help you? I'm guessing not.

If you have a lot of debt, don't worry about your food truck dream, it will come into reality eventually. The business and your ideas are not going anywhere.

Having taken the time to read this book up to this point says you are serious about moving forward, so if you have a lot of accumulated debt, adding the start-up cost of a food truck or trailer is not the correct answer, it will only make it harder for you to keep up financially, especially with the small amount of income that comes at the startup phase of this venture. To proceed further could automatically set you up for failure. Don't let the excitement of starting a food truck blind you from the tasks that need your attention now. Take time to assess your situation and work on anything hindering your finances. Taking on these debts head-on now will allow you a smoother start-up by having less pressure to make a large sum of money to cover these away in the future. Get comfortable with your personal finances to move forward with a fresh start to your new business.

Also keep in mind:

You may not make the money you had hoped for right away, so be careful with your expectations.

You don't want to tack on more debt that will allow money to create even more stress in your life.

Adding more financial burdens to your life will not allow you to focus fully on your food truck.

Why? Because you may have to keep working your day job just to keep up with paying your bills.

If you're in that situation, it will leave you with very little time to focus on your food truck.

You want as fresh of a start as possible.

You will find enough pressure and stress in this line of business, so you don't want to add to it. Having added pressure will only take away your passion to proceed.

Only you know what needs immediate attention in your life to make this venture a reality. You will know when it's time to move forward… one day you will get to walk away from your day job. It will happen, but it will happen organically.

What if you're not good at money management?

Consider taking a course and getting your financial knowledge in order. Running and operating a food truck will be yet another learning curve for you to learn how to reinvest in your business while still paying yourself. Remember, just because you are making money doesn't mean it's all yours to pocket or to go out and spend it.

Other things to consider:

Have separate bank accounts for your personal and business spending. That will help a lot when it comes to filing income tax returns at the end of the year.

When setting up your budget, put money aside to cover your general weekly needs and restock groceries.

Try to set aside a 'rainy-day fund' for maintenance and unexpected emergencies. They will happen.

There are two things certain in life: death and taxes.

Put money aside for taxes. Remember that your card swiping system can be set up to add taxes so that your customers pay taxes after every purchase.

Also, put money aside for licensing fees and enough to cover any insurance that must be renewed.

TIP: *Consider putting aside any tips you make to help pay for all of the above.*

This is an example of my business account.

Business Checking:

Here, any money that I make gets deposited and is used for business purchases and related expenses only. I also use it to make transfers to the accounts below.

(*These can be in one account or separate accounts.*)

Savings 1 (Taxes)

Here, I transfer my taxes from monthly swipes but also add an extra percentage of income for federal tax and my professional tax preparer's rate.

Savings 2 (Profits)

Here, I transfer my tips and an extra percentage of income for future growth. I do not touch this account.

Savings 3 (Emergency Fund)

Here, I transfer $100.00 a month for emergencies and unexpected maintenance.

All this may sound overwhelming but trust me when I say that once you are in the business flow, you will get a better look at what you need to put aside. You will also see that you can make more than enough to pay for these necessities and yourself from your very own food truck.

The money you put aside may seem small at first but will start to accumulate quickly. The feeling of being prepared for any unexpected or expected expense that may arise is priceless and takes away all unnecessary stress that comes with it.

§§§§§

Summary:

- Don't let the excitement of starting a food truck blind you from tasks that need your attention now.
- Just because you are making money does not mean it's all yours to pocket and spend it all at once.

- There are two things certain in life, death and taxes.
- The feeling of being prepared for any unexpected or expected expenses that may arise is priceless and takes away all unnecessary stress that comes with it.

Conclusion

I've provided you with some valuable information, but do not try and accomplish all of the above overnight. This book is meant to be used as a stepping-stone as you pass through each stage in the food truck business.

The advice in these pages will help you avoid the costly mistakes I made, making your food truck career a smoother and more prosperous journey by giving you the extra confidence and information that is needed for you to get started and not move into this venture blindly.

This book is meant to provide you with ideas that will assist you in generating income consistently, but most importantly, to make sure you have fun on your journey in the food truck business, regardless of any mistake you make along the way. You're sure to face challenges that I haven't experienced, but it's important to face them head-on as I did and keep moving forward.

Of this, I am certain...*the rewards and experiences that come with the jump are well worth the ride.*

Welcome to the food truck life.

I would love to hear from anyone who has read this book and see how your truck is coming along.

Feel free to send a personal message on Facebook or Instagram to The Blacktop Grill and let me know how this book has helped you. I will happily become one of your first followers on social media and keep up with you on your food truck journey.

About the Author

Originally from Yuma, Arizona, and now residing in Tucson, Gabe Ceniceros is both a food creator and a food lover … a musician, a loving father and husband, and proud owner of The Blacktop Grill.

Gabe's restaurant career began at the age of sixteen working for both large food chains and privately owned restaurants. Gabe has worked in and knows all facets of the restaurant industry from fast food to casual to fine dining and everything in between. He has accumulated more than 20 years of experience in the industry.

For ten of those years, Gabe has been a food truck owner and is now also a restaurant owner.

Gabe is considered an expert in his field. His visions for The Blacktop Grill keep extending to new heights.

His journey began with an old food cart in 2014 that was held together with duct tape. Since then, he has had an amazing journey of growth. What makes his story so interesting is that he has gone from an old, run-down food cart to a full-fledged brick-and-mortar restaurant in just seven short years! Along with his personal growth, The Blacktop Grill has garnered award-winning food recognition and has been featured in countless numbers of publications and podcasts.

Through the years, Gabe has earned expertise in the food truck and restaurant industry. During the journey, he has accumulated some very valuable lessons.

Gabe is now ready to pay it forward by sharing his wealth of priceless knowledge with anyone looking to become an entrepreneur and jump into the exciting, yet challenging world of the food truck industry.

The Blacktop Grill, Tucson AZ

Breaking diets since 2014, The Blacktop Grill is known for specializing in gourmet comfort food.

Our menu consists of decadent hotdogs, tacos, quesadillas, and an overall menu that we describe as, 'Sonoran with a twist.'

We take authentic meals and flavors and combine them to make a unique and exciting culinary experience.

As food lovers, we personally explore locally owned restaurants in every city we visit. We seek those that stand out, that are fun and different, and offer delicious options that only locals can recommend.

Our Vision for The Blacktop Grill is to be this for the people… *we strive to be the fun eats for food lovers wanting different and exciting foods.*

People who give you their food give you their heart.
(Cesar Chavez)

Michael J.

24 109 48 Elite '20

Sep 20, 2019 9:39 PM

The Black Top Grill gets five stars alone for the customer service...but than you try the unique flavors on the menu and realize this truly is a five-star food truck!

www.ingramcontent.com/pod-product-compliance
Ingram Content Group UK Ltd.
Pitfield, Milton Keynes, MK11 3LW, UK
UKHW062253290726
14090UKWH00017B/667

9 798894 438795